John Chapman's
TRANSPORT PAINTINGS

John Chapman's
TRANSPORT PAINTINGS

IN ASSOCIATION WITH

J.L. Chapman (Studios) Ltd

First published in Great Britain in 2011

British Library Cataloguing-in-Publication Data
A CIP record for this title is available from the British Library

ISBN 978 1 906690 11 3

HALSTAR
Halsgrove House,
Ryelands Business Park,
Bagley Road, Wellington, Somerset TA21 9PZ
Tel: 01823 653777   Fax: 01823 216796
email: sales@halsgrove.com

Part of the Halsgrove group of companies
Information on all Halsgrove titles is available at: www.halsgrove.com

Printed in Italy by Grafiche Flaminia

~ Foreword ~

This is the second book of my paintings published by Halsgrove. The first one concentrated on Lancashire the county of my birth and where I still live. The first book contained details of my Lancashire roots and how the county had influenced my work.

As a boy transport held a fascination for me, especially cars. This was not unusual in the early 1950s when most families particularly the ones I knew didn't own one. They were looked on as a great luxury and a ride in a car even for a short distance was something I looked forward to with eager anticipation. A good friend of my parents, in fact he was my godfather, did own a car and quite an unusual one. It was a Lanchester, which was black as were so many cars, but it had automatic transmission: this was a necessity for my godfather as he only had one arm. I remember one trip in the Lanchester when my godfather tried to find out how fast the old girl would go. There is a hill coming out of Preston on the main Blackburn road. It drops down to the River Ribble and is now in a 30 mile an hour zone. Well, on that day I think we hit 65 miles an hour.

I was born in Blackburn, Lancashire in 1946 and by 1951 I was attending St Silas's Primary School which was about 200 yards from where I lived on New Bank Road. There was a row of shops opposite the school just lower down from where I lived. The first one was a fish and chip shop, very important, but the second shop on the row was Mr Lucas's toy shop. Although most of the shop contained sports equipment, tennis rackets and cricket bats, for me the main attraction was a fine collection of Dinky toys and Hornby 00 train sets. The train sets were well beyond my parents' means, but at about three shillings and sixpence the purchase of a brand new Dinky toy was a reality, provided I saved my one shilling a week pocket money. My mother used to clean for a gent who owned a large garage on the main Preston road. This kind gentleman used to give me the run of the place, and I would stride about as though I

owned it, health and safety did not apply in those days, and to cap it all, I would come away with half a crown to add to my shilling, enough for another Dinky toy.

Well cars may have been my main interest but my passion was drawing. I just could not stop. My big influence was my brother Michael who was seven years older. He was a very talented artist producing imaginary drawings of cars, aircraft, and tanks. I would sit watching him for hours and the fact that he was left handed fascinated me even more.

Apart from the rare trip in a motor car our main method of transport was by bus or coach and the occasional train. Blackburn Corporation ran a fleet of green-livered Guy double deckers. Unfortunately, I just missed the old trams as they ended in 1949, and sadly none were preserved, though I seem to remember riding in a vehicle with wooden seats similar to the ones on the trams. The tram tracks remained long after the trams disappeared and some sections could be seen up until recent times. Longer trips would mean taking a Ribble bus or coach; these operated on a number of routes to coastal resorts such as Southport, Blackpool or Morecambe. They sported a distinctive deep red and cream livery. The express coaches were cream and they all carried Preston registrations.

My parents were very keen ramblers and belonged to the Blackburn Ramblers Club. Every Sunday I would accompany them on what seemed to me to be very long walks on average about ten miles. We regularly used Ribble buses to get us into the surrounding countryside to start our walk. On some occasions we would use rambler's excursion trains to the Peak District and the Yorkshire Dales. All these early train journeys were steam hauled. I can recall the first time a D.M.U. [Diesel Multiple Unit] was used and it was a great novelty not to have a steam locomotive pulling our train.

Family holidays were taken during the annual Wake's week in July. All the mills and indeed the whole town would virtually close around this time which would be in the mid 1950s. We stayed at a remote farm which was situated in the Duddon Valley a part of the Lake District. The journey would entail three changes of train before arriving at Millom on the Cumberland coast. There the farmer would meet us in his old Ford Pick-Up. Mum would squeeze inside and I would ride outside with the cases and perhaps a couple of sheep dogs. This journey would take forever as the farmer would insist on stopping in order to count his Herdwick sheep. Fortunately, he didn't fall asleep. Our holidays to the Ayrshire coast in Scotland were no less simple. First there would be a local train to Hellifield, a remote and always windy station across the border in Yorkshire. Here we would catch the express from Leeds to Glasgow. This would be hauled by a Royal Scot locomotive or later a Gresley A3

Pacific could be used. We would alight at Kilmarnock where we would board an old red double decker bus which was destined for Stranraer. After a two hour bone-jarring ride we would alight at our destination just south of Girvan. We stayed in a cottage almost on the shore, sometimes in a wood cabin and once in an old bus minus its wheels.

Having failed my eleven plus examination I found myself at Bangor Street Secondary Modern School. It did have a couple of good things in its favour – a very good art teacher called Peter Shackleton, and at lunchtime they showed British transport films. Peter Shackleton had achieved celebrity status by selling one of his paintings to Barbara Castle who was the M.P. for Blackburn. For this achievement he was given coverage on the local television news. He must have recognised that I had some artistic talent as he arranged for me to attend Saturday morning classes at the Blackburn College of Art. One of the big highlights during my time at Bangor Street School was a trip to Paris. Therefore I visited the Louvre long before our own National Gallery. On the journey home whilst at Victoria Station and waiting around for a coach to transfer us to Euston, I started train spotting. Many of my school pals were into the hobby so I had a bit of catching up to do. Another school trip which all the spotters eagerly anticipated was to Crewe Locomotive Works and both North and South Motive Power Depots, otherwise known as the sheds. Although by this time diesel locomotives were being built at the works there were many steam locomotives being serviced and repaired. By now I had started to paint railway subjects and I still have many of them. They are rather weak on the technical side but full of drama with plenty of smoke and steam covering up the tricky things such as wheels and valve gear. My brother was now working on the railway as a booking clerk and I can remember him bringing home some posters by my favourite railway artist Terence Cuneo. I do not know what happened to them as they would be worth a small fortune now.

I left school in 1961 and on New Year's Day 1962 I started working as a lay out artist in the Advertising Department of Blackburn's local newspaper *The Lancashire Evening Telegraph*. It may have said 'artist' in the job title but there wasn't anything artistic about cutting up other people's illustrations courtesy of Madison Avenue and pasting them onto a board and dreaming of a suitable slogan. I think my lack of enthusiasm showed itself, and I was politely shown the door.

So in 1964 I became a full time art student attending classes in the same building I had spent school-days Saturday mornings. As well as continuing to paint railway subjects I fancied being a car stylist, so I wrote off to all the major car manufacturers in the naïve notion that they would offer me a job. The response wasn't very encouraging: apparently you needed lots of qualifications and an 0 Level in art wasn't going to do it. The head of the art school was James Dolby, himself a fine artist, and he was instrumental in securing me an interview for a job as a technical illustrator for a local engineering company. The outcome was successful and although illustrating spare parts manuals for excavators wasn't exactly styling next year's Jaguar, it was a job were I would be employing my drawing skills.

My brother was still living at home but now he had a car: it was a two tone black and cream MK 1 Ford Consul and it cost all of £55. Virtually every weekend we were out photographing steam trains. Michael had given up drawing in favour of photography. I recall we once spent all night in that Consul parked by the west coast main line on Shap, so as to make sound recordings of the overnight trains as they stormed the bank.

By 1968 steam was coming to an end and so was my time as a technical illustrator. Rumours were true that JCB Engineering were negotiating a take over of Chaseside Engineering and come July 1968 I became redundant. But this was not before Anthony Bamford, the son of Joe Bamford founder of JCB, had commissioned me to paint a picture of his MGB sports car, which he had entered in a European Sport Car Series. The car like the excavators was bright yellow, and it was due to having a selection of my work hanging on the walls of the Drawing Office, that caught the eye of Anthony Bamford.

So the decision was made that I would become a full time artist. I had never really stopped painting and with my portfolio full of paintings I set forth to the Manchester Galleries. I had various degrees of success; one in particular was J. Davey & Son on Bridge Street. It was a shop which sold art materials and did picture framing. Now whether Mr Davey was a railway enthusiast of whether he recognised a niche market is unclear, but he bought several of my

paintings there and then. I was an extremely happy professional artist as I travelled back to Blackburn clutching a cheque for all of £30.

A few weeks later I returned to Davey & Son to see if anything had been sold and if he would like any more paintings. The answer to both these questions was yes, not only that but he had secured me some commissions as well.

Although railway paintings were my main staple I started to branch out into marine subjects and Victorian street scenes complete with Hansom cabs and horse-drawn buses and trams. Around this time I acquired my first car, a second hand Triumph Herald in midnight blue and I shared it with Michael who was still working on the railway, but becoming disenchanted and in need of a change. This came in the mid 1970s when he decided to leave Blackburn and move to the north of Scotland.

I continued to refine my art and never stopped painting almost fearing if I did stop I may not be able to start again. My only holidays were trips to London to visit the galleries and any special exhibitions. I would usually stay with my auntie in Reading and travel up to Paddington every day. I did have a change once and got on a train going in the opposite direction to Oxford. Viewing great works of art was part of my education. I would stand for ages in front of the Turners at the Tate Gallery. One of my favourite museums is the Science Museum and the main attraction for me was a huge painting of Waterloo Station by Terence Cuneo. I still consider this to be one of Britain's greatest paintings. I would also visit small private galleries in Mayfair. It was always a dream that one day I would have my work hanging on those hallowed walls. Little did I know that I would not have long to wait.

I first met Keith Lee in the early 1970s. A few years later we met up again and formed a business partnership. Up to then I had been enjoying my painting and making a living but I felt that I needed something more and Keith offered me the opportunity of an exhibition at W. H. Patterson's Gallery in Mayfair. This was my dream come true, the year was 1977, and the date of my exhibition was April 1978 and they would need 42 paintings. Well, I had two which was a start. So in order to produce 40 paintings in a year would mean working solidly for 12 months with no days off. The exhibition was entitled 'The Nostalgic World of J. L. Chapman' and of the 42 paintings exhibited well over 30 were sold on the preview night. Many more exhibitions followed including some in my home town of Blackburn but nothing could compare with that first one man show.

During the 1980s I started using acrylics and I still use them extensively. It's a medium which suits my style and enables me to put in all the detail which transport subjects demand. Even so, I have recently returned to oils on canvas, and for a complete change I still do water colours. I paint nearly every day and if I am not painting or drawing I'll be out gathering material at classic car shows, steam rallies or at one of the preserved railways this country is now blessed with, and all with one aim, to recreate in paint a gentler and more evocative age.

Fordson Thames Truck – Mersey Tunnel

King George V opened The Queensway Tunnel in July 1934, taking traffic under the River Mersey between Liverpool and Birkenhead. Various commercial vehicles can be seen emerging from the entrance in Liverpool including a Thames Fordson and a Morris van. On the left a Jaguar is about to enter the tunnel.

Great Victoria Street, Belfast

A McCreary tram No.409 passes the terminus of the Great Northern Railway of Ireland. Sadly, this building was demolished about 1970 to make way for the Europa Hotel. A Ford V8 Pilot and an Austin as well as a horse and cart can be seen on the street.

Sunderland Tram

A Sunderland tram car trundles down Bridge Street. The Wearmouth Bridge was the only road link between the two halves of Sunderland. The railway bridge can also been seen running alongside. A Humber Pullman and a Fordson share road space with the tram.

David Brown Cropmaster Tractor

This particular tractor was seen at an event near Ormskirk in Lancashire organised by the Northern Counties Heavy Horse Working Society. Both horses and tractors were demonstrating ploughing. For a layman such as myself there was no discernable difference in the furrows, only the time it took to finish their respective working areas, and I suppose this was why the horse had to give way to the tractor. Approximately sixty thousand Cropmasters were manufactured from 1948 to 1954. The tractor's engine produced 35 b.h.p with a top speed of 18 m.p.h.

Leeds Trams Montage

In this montage two Leeds trams can be seen operating in the city during the 1950s. On the left a 'Horsfield' car passes under the railway bridge at the junction of Briggate, Swinegate, Bridge End, and Call Lane. The tram on the right is a 'Feltham' car in New Market Street.

Glasgow Trams Montage

On the left a former Liverpool car passes along Argyle Street with Central Station in the background. The two trams on the right are a Standard car and a Coronation car in a typical Glasgow street of the 1950s.

Classic Black

During the 1960s and '70s black was not a popular colour for cars. Nowadays it's much more popular and on these 1950s classics you have to admit that it does show off the chrome! Models clockwise are a Triumph Roadster, a Morris, a Standard Vanguard and a rear view of a Triumph Mayflower.

Classics at Gawthorpe Hall

A line up of classic cars during a rally in the grounds of Gawthorpe Hall near Burnley. They include a rear view of a Lea Francis and a Jaguar XK 140. Partially hidden are a Rolls Royce and a red MG.

British Classics

A montage of British cars from the 1950s, including a Riley, a Sunbeam Talbot, a rear view of a Jaguar and two Austins, a Somerset and an A40.

Classic Montage

Rear views of a Morris, and a Triumph Roadster. Front view of a two-tone Vauxhall Convertible.

Sauchiehall Street, Glasgow

This view of Sauchiehall Street around 1950 is from the roof of the La Scala Cinema looking east. A Coronation tram is followed by a Standard car. The street has now become pedestrianised but many of the original buildings remain.

Steam Rollers at St Michaels

Two steam rollers get admiring glances at the Annual Steam Fair at St Michaels on Wyre in Lancashire. Both are Aveling and Porter 10 ton rollers and built in the early twentieth century. Behind them can be seen a couple of period vans in which the engine-men would have lived whilst doing road repairs.

Manchester Trolley Bus

An Asley Crossley Trolley Bus on the Ashton route stands at the Portland Street Terminus. The Manchester Trolley Bus system ended in December 1966. The motor bus then reigned supreme until the Metrolink trams appeared in 1992.

Gladstone Dock, Liverpool

A steamship is at the quayside and centre stage is a Thames Trader lorry awaiting its next duty whilst a Saddle Tank locomotive belonging to the Mersey Docks & Harbour Board steams by. A scene common in the 1950s but now totally disappeared.

The Port of Liverpool

This rather idealised view of Liverpool Docks is set in the early fifties. The Liver Building appears above the warehouses giving it a distinct Liverpudlian feel and the sunlit River Mersey complete with tug boats and Birkenhead in the distance sets the scene. Since this time the docks have undergone a radical transformation with container ships and bulk carriers taking over from the humble tramp steamer. Much of dockland became derelict, but fortunately the Albert Dock together with its Grade One listed buildings was saved, and has been transformed into a major tourist attraction.

Sheffield 1950s

This is Weedon Street in the mid 1950s. A Roberts's car No.507 in the distinctive cream and blue striped livery prepares to depart for Leopold Street in the city centre. A Scammell Mechanical Horse can be seen in the distance, and a Vauxhall Velox is parked on the right. The steel works has been demolished and also the terraced houses on the left. Sheffield lost its trams in 1960, but you can still ride on Sheffield's Last Tram at the Crich Tramway Village in Derbyshire.

Camden – Engine Shed 1950s

Just a mile north of Euston is Camden Engine Shed which serviced and turned all the express locomotives for the trains from Euston to the North. From the left we can see a rear view of a Jinty 0-6-0 Tank Engine. Next a 'Jubilee' Class has the ash removed from its smoke box. In the centre stands 'Corporation' Class Pacific No.46245 *City of London* and next is 'Royal Scot' Class No. 46148 *The Manchester Regiment*. Camden Shed closed to steam in 1963 and was demolished in 1964.

Ingrow Station Trolley

A little cameo on the preserved railway station of Ingrow which is part of the Keighley & Worth Valley Railway in Yorkshire. Milk churns and large trunks were all part of the railway picture in days gone by, but such scenes are re-created on many of Britain's preserved railways.

Tower Bridge

This is no doubt one of London's best known landmarks, built in 1894 in the Gothic style. On the left is the Tower of London, parts of which date back to the eleventh century. The Routemaster bus dates from the 1950s and was the last bus to be designed by London Transport for use in the capital. They were built to last for 15 years but some went on to still be running after 40 years. This particular example is on its way from Shoreditch to Dulwich. The black cab so typical of London is now a common sight throughout Britain, but like the Routemaster these will eventually disappear from our streets.

Blackpool circa 1955

A 'Jubilee' Class locomotive No 45697 *Achilles* departs from Blackpool Central Station circa 1955. The station closed in 1965 and became a car park. In the background Blackpool Tower constructed in 1894 rises to a height of 520 feet.

The Pie Man Cometh

Holland's Pies of Baxenden, which is just outside Accrington, are famous throughout the North of England. The Bedford delivery van with its distinctive livery has been restored and often appears at historic vehicle rallies. It is seen here passing the Accrington Fire & Police Station in Manchester Road in the 1950s. The church tower, part of the Wesley Chapel, was demolished in the '60s after it became unsafe. A Vauxhall and a Wolseley share the road.

Steam Hall G.W.R. Locos

This painting depicts ex. G.W.R. locos in shed; a loco is being turned manually. Roundhouses were common to all regions and this one is at Old Oak Common in London. They were the cathedrals of the steam age.

Portland Place, London

Portland Place is the home of Broadcasting House. The distinctive Art Deco building dates from 1932 and was designed by G. Val Myer with sculptural elements by Eric Gill. On the right stands All Souls' Church. This early 1950s' view shows a typical London taxi loaded with luggage. Behind it and an Austin Somerset followed by a London R T double decker bus.

St Mark's Road, Preston

This Lancashire street scene with its cobbles and terraced houses is situated near the railway line to Blackpool from Preston. The signal box perched high up on an embankment is called Maudland Viaduct. A Vauxhall saloon climbs up the steep street and a train approaches from the Blackpool direction.

Engine Drivers Montage

These studies of footplate crew were all based on scenes seen on preserved railways such as the East Lancashire Railway and North Yorkshire Moors Railway. They all sport the traditional grease top cap.

Woodcock Takes on Water

The footplate crew, engine driver and his fireman stand alongside their 'steed', an A4 Pacific 60029 *Woodcock* before taking their train on its northbound journey.

Isle of Man Loco Montage

Four Beyer Peacock 2-4-0 Tank Engines belonging to the 3 foot gauge Isle of Man Railway are featured here in three different liveries. The line runs from Douglas to Port Erin in the south-west of the island.

I.O.M. Loco No.10 *C.H. Wood* **at Port Erin**

A Beyer Peacock 2.4.0 Tank rests at Port Erin having brought its train from Douglas. The engine No.10 is named *C.H. Wood*.

Express Steam

Featured in this montage: top left, the fireman of a Stanier Black 5 leans out of the cab window; shed staff prepare an A1 Pacific; and detail of two Gresley A4 Pacifics.

Bellerophon

This is one of the oldest preserved steam locos still operating and is seen here in the shed yard at Haworth Station on the Keighley & Worth Valley Railway.

Kyle of Lochalsh

A Clan goods locomotive is about to depart for Inverness. A McBraynes steamer also gets in on the act. The mountains of the Isle of Skye can be seen in the background, circa 1947.

The Golden Arrow

The famous boat train to Paris is about to depart from Victoria Station in London. The locomotive is a 'Merchant Navy' Pacific designed by Bulleid and introduced in 1941. It is seen in its early blue livery. The coaches are Pullman with their chocolate and cream livery.

'Pug' at the Pool

These small Saddle Tank locomotives were affectionately known as 'Pugs' and belonged to the Mersey Docks and Harbour Board, which had an extensive railway, part of which ran underneath the overhead railway known as the Docker's Umbrella. Traffic waits to cross as Pug No. 51204 hauls goods wagons covered with tarpaulin sheets. Traffic includes a tram on Route 44 and a Vauxhall saloon. Horses could still be seen hauling goods into the 1950s. The poster on one of the steel columns advertises cruises on the *Doric*. The overhead railway closed in December 1956 and trams finished in 1957.

The *Lion*

The 150th anniversary of the Liverpool & Manchester Railway took place in 1980, and to celebrate this, the locomotive *Lion* was steamed. This locomotive was built in Leeds in 1838 and had a very eventful career including a starring role in the 1952 film *The Titfield Thunderbolt*. Here it is seen hauling a replica open carriage at The Museum of Science & Industry in Manchester.

Cleaning the Smoke-Box of a Castle

Maintaining a steam locomotive was often a filthy and unpleasant job. At the Old Oak Common Stage an ex. G.W.R. 'Castle' class Locomotive has its smoke-box cleaned out after a day's working.

Dickson Road, Blackpool 1960

A Blackpool 'Balloon' tram stops outside the Odeon Cinema on its journey from North Station to Fleetwood. Built by English Electric these double-decker trams were built in the mid 1930s.

The trams on this route stopped in October 1963. Cars parked on the left include a Rover and an Austin Somerset. A Sunbeam Talbot heads in the opposite direction. The Odeon Cinema was built in 1939 with seating for three thousand.

Crane Locomotive, Hodbarrow Mines

I don't know the history of this unusual engine. I came across it and several sister engines at an abandoned siding at the Hodbarrow Iron Ore Mines, near Millom about 1960. I was visiting my grandmother who lived not far away at the coastal village of Haverigg. I think all the locomotives found homes at industrial museums and though I haven't re-visited the site I would imagine it has all been re-developed.

Dinorwic Slate Quarries

The mountains of Wales contain vast quantities of slate and during the Industrial Revolution a great demand for housing created a need for slate roofs. The Dinorwic Quarries were one of the largest producers of slate in the world. Many of these narrow gauge locomotives now operate on tourist lines such as the Ffestiniog.

Talbot Square, Blackpool

Talbot Square is the centre of Blackpool; in the shadow on the left is the Town Hall. The single-deck streamlined tram dates from the 1930s and is destined for Royal Oak via Marton. A St Anne's bus is on the right. The Promenade and North Pier can be seen in the distance. A Jaguar MK V is parked outside the Town Hall.

Pantograph Tram at Fleetwood

Built by English Electric in 1928 the single deck Pantograph cars had a unique quality and were used on the route from Blackpool up the coast to Fleetwood. This one is passing the Knott-End Ferry Terminus and a fishing trawler can be seen making its way up the River Wyre to the port. The white building in the distance is the Life Boat House.

The Boat Car

The boat cars arrived in Blackpool in 1934 and proved an instant success especially in fine weather with visitors wanting to see interesting parts of the town while enjoying the sunshine. This scene set in the 1950s shows a boat car proceeding down the Promenade and no doubt heading for the Pleasure Beach on South Shore. A motor coach heads towards the Tower followed by an Austin Somerset. Parked at the kerb side is one of Blackpool's horse drawn landaus waiting for its next customers.

Bittern

Gresley A4 Pacific 60019 *Bittern* climbs through the cutting towards the Forth Bridge on the last leg of its journey from Aberdeen to Edinburgh in the mid 1960s. This painting was based on a photograph my brother Michael took. His photographs of railways have been an inspiration for my own work. *Bittern* was saved from the scrap yard and can be seen on steam specials.

Oakworth Station G.N.R. 0.6.0 Tank loco, Keighley and Worth Valley Railway.

Rolls Royce and Bentley owners meeting, Stonyhurst, Lancs.

Birmingham New Street 1950s

A Patriot loco 45503 *The Royal Leicestershire Regiment* awaits departure as a Black 5 arrives on an excursion.

William Bowker's Thornycroft truck at Church near Blackburn 1930s.

A Blackburn Corporation tram heads under the Infirmary Railway Bridge on its way towards Darwen circa 1947.

Sheffield's last tram, a Roberts Car No. 510, picks up passengers at Crich Tramway Museum, Derbyshire. The cars are a Triumph Roadster and a Morris.

Whitbread Brewery Horse-Drawn Dray Crosses Tower Bridge

Out delivering beer a Whitbread Brewery horse-drawn dray crosses Tower Bridge circa 1950s. Whitbread was founded in 1742 and finished brewing in 2001. On the left is the Tower of London built in 1078 for William the Conqueror. It was both palace and prison as well as a fortress and the Traitor's Gate opened direct on to the Thames. Tower Bridge was completed in 1894. It is a twin bascule bridge and can be opened in 1½ minutes and there is a permanent footway 142 ft. above the Thames. The total length of the bridge is half a mile.

LNER A3 Pacific Loco No.4472 *Flying Scotsman* pays a visit to the East Lancashire Railway. Seen at Ramsbottom Station.

The Coronation Scot hauled by Stanier Pacific 6229 *Duchess of Hamilton*. Circa 1939.

Lancashire & Yorkshire 0-6-0 loco No. 52322 on shed having just taken on a tender full of coal from the tower in the background.

Shap Banker Fowler 2-6-4 Tank loco gives a helping hand to a north-bound freight.

The driver oiling round the motion of a Stanier Black 5.

Gresley A4 Pacific Loco 60007 *Sir Nigel Gresley*. This locomotive reached 112 m.p.h in 1959.

L & Y Railway 0-4-0 Pug Saddle Tank No. 51218 is inspected having run hot approaching Oakworth on the Keighley & Worth Valley Railway.

Bolton Departure

A Hughes/Fowler Class 6P5F 2-6-0 No. 42901 departs from Bolton Trinity Street Station bound for Manchester, and in all probability could be a rambler's excursion to the Peak District. A Stanier Black 5 heads in the opposite direction towards the station. Here the line splits, one route going to Preston and the other to Blackburn. Beyond the station building is the Town Hall Clock Tower. The clock tower on the right and above the train belongs to the station. The station buildings were demolished in 1987, but the clock tower was spared and incorporated into the new building.

A Stanier Class 5 Locomotive at Great Harwood Junction Blackburn, on an excursion from Blackpool back to Yorkshire 1966.

The motion of L.N.E.R. K3 showing Walschaerts valve gear.

Mostyn Street, Llandudno 1950s

An ex-Bournemouth tramcar heads down Mostyn Street towards Colwyn Bay. A Rover and Wolseley are parked either side, and dominating the background is the Great Orme. I first visited Llandudno as a schoolboy in the 1950s. I arrived by steamer from Liverpool. Sadly, the trams had finished by then but at least the Great Orme Tramway was operating, as it is today.

Waterfoot 1950s

Between Bacup and Rawtenstall in Lancashire's Rossendale Valley lies Waterfoot. Here we see a Lancashire and Yorkshire 0-6-0 heading towards the station and coming towards us, having just left the station, is a tank engine and two coaches, destination Bacup. A local double-decker bus heads away from us and a Morris 1000 van is behind. A Holland's Pie van, and a Hillman Minx heads towards Bacup.

Churchgate, Bolton

This is the junction of Deansgate and Bradshawgate in the heart of Bolton in the 1950s. Many of the buildings remain but you can no longer drive down Churchgate as it is now pedestrianised. The large building with the clock tower is Preston's Jewellery Store. From 1908 to 1944 the ball mounted on a steel mast gave Bolton its accurate time. It was connected by landline to Greenwich Observatory and precisely at 10.00 am every morning the ball dropped ten feet. Vehicles on Churchgate include a Bedford 10 cwt van, a Vauxhall Velox and an Austin Cambridge.

Wigan Pier – Service Station

Much has been written about Wigan Pier but it did actually exist. It was a coal tippler on a raised part of the canal towpath. Equally famous are Uncle Joe's Mint Balls which are made in Wigan. A large advertisement for this product on the gable end of a house by the main London to Glasgow railway line made sure everyone knew about this legendary confectionery. Parked at the garage on the left is a Morris Tourer, as a salesman describes its finer points to a potential customer. A Ford V8 Pilot and a Hillman Minx fill their tanks. Notice the ex-Army truck converted to a breakdown wagon. This scene dates from just after the Second World War.

Southern Pacifics

Two of Bulleid's express locomotives raise steam in Nine Elm Engine Shed in London. 34031 *Torrington* is a rebuilt 'West Country' Class Loco. 34071 *601 Squadron* is a 'Battle of Britain Class' loco, in un-rebuilt condition. It was seeing these types of engine on a school trip to Paris via London and Folkestone that introduced me to the train-spotting hobby. After my school days I became more interested in photography and as locomotives were being scrapped in large numbers spotting became a bit pointless.

Vintage Bentley

I can't claim to have much knowledge of vintage Bentleys, so I can't offer any details as to what model I've painted here, only to say it's from the 1920s and is painted in British Racing Green the only colour for a car with such a sporting pedigree.

Local Train – Lancashire Landscape from Train

This is a totally imaginary view but one I've seen many times as I peered out of a carriage window, mainly to see what engine was at the front. In this case it's an ex L.M.S. Tank Engine with a rake of maroon coaches. The terraced houses, mills and evocative posters are part of the fabric of 1950s industrial Lancashire and of course it's a dull wet day. The nearest you could get to experiencing a scene such as this is to take a ride on the East Lancashire Railway between Bury and Rawtenstall.

On the Turntable

Designed by Sir Nigel Gresley and introduced in 1935 the A4 Pacific locomotives were the ultimate in streamlined engines. This particular example is 60019 *Bittern* and is preserved as a working example. Its sister engine *Mallard*, claimed the world record for steam at 126 m.p.h in July 1938. *Mallard* can be seen on display at the National Railway Museum at York.

Lancaster Castle Station

A northbound express is ready to depart from Lancaster Station and the engine crew are eager to be off. A group of train-spotters are admiring the 'Royal Scot' Class Locomotive 46115 *Scots Guardsman* which has recently been restored to working order and is once more working special steam excursions. I spent many a happy day on the end of this platform watching and photographing steam trains. With a change of trains at Preston it could easily take two hours to reach Lancaster from Blackburn but it was worth it to watch expresses such as the Caledonian roar through on its way south.

Blackburn Station – Platform 2 – 1960

The Lancashire & Yorkshire train shed at Blackburn looked almost cathedral-like and as a child I remember starting many journeys from there, usually to Blackpool, sometimes a rambler's excursion to the Yorkshire Dales and once as a schoolboy all the way to Kilmarnock. The train indicator boards were still in use up to the 1970s. A model of the Isle of Man Steam Ship MV *Viking* in its glass case can be seen just beyond the seated man. The whole station was re-developed a few years ago, so nothing now remains of this scene today.

Manchester Exchange Station Departure

Stanier Class 6P5F 'Jubilee' No. 45698 departs from platform 3 of Manchester Exchange Station on a train for Liverpool. A 'Patriot' No. 45517 heads towards Victoria. Exchange Station was built in 1884 as a result of congestion at Victoria. The stations being connected by the 2,194 feet long platform 11, which was the longest in the country.

Bank Hay Street and Central Station

Bank Hay Street Central Station Blackpool 1950s; on the right is the New Inn and Central Hotel. A Burlingham-bodied Leyland Titan stands at the bus stop. A Ford V8 Pilot and a Standard Vanguard complete the scene.

The Keighley & Worth Valley Railway

This 5-mile branch line between Keighley and Oxenhope is the second oldest former B.R. preserved line. It has been running trains since 1968 and has become well known through such films as *The Railway Children* which was filmed on location. Here we see 1VA77 Class 2 2-6-2 Tank No. 41241 on a train near Oakworth. This locomotive has now been painted black but in the early days of the railway it sported crimson lake livery.

Blackburn Road Accrington in the 1950s

A Guy Arab single decker in the distinctive Accrington livery pulls away from its stop and crosses Leslie Hore-Belisha's, great contribution to road safety, the Zebra Crossing. Originally the crossings were marked out by studs and yellow glass beacons. These were later replaced by painted aluminium globes. The crossings got their stripes in 1951 and in 1952 the beacons began to wink. The impressive building on the left is the Town Hall and further along is the Market Hall. A MK 5 Jaguar follows a double-decker bus and approaching we see a Bedford CA van and a Humber Super-Snipe.

The Flying Scotsman

This is another of my early railway paintings and shows the *Flying Scotsman* Express leaving Copenhagen Tunnel on its journey from London King's Cross to Edinburgh during the late 1930s. The famous steam locomotive 4472 an A3 Pacific designed by Sir Nigel Gresley is hauling the train.

Manchester – Corporation Street 1950s

Corporation Street was created in the mid nineteenth century to improve communications between central Manchester and the Cheetham Hill area and to relieve congestion in the Market Place and along Millgate. This busy looking east scene includes three Manchester Corporation Leyland double deckers. On the left coming into the scene is a late '30s Rolls Royce, an Austin Somerset, coming toward us is a pre-war Vauxhall Saloon and a British Railways 25 CWT Commer parcel van.

Glasgow

A Glasgow Standard Tram emerges from the 'Heilandman's Umbrella' beneath Glasgow Central Station in the 1950s. The car is an Austin A90 Atlantic; it came out in the late 1940s and was specifically aimed at the American market. Though it was unsuccessful in finding buyers, today it is a much prized classic and really quite rare.

Liverpool – Castle Street – Late 1940s

This is a view of Castle Street looking towards the Town Hall and the junction of Water Street. This scene is set soon after the Second World War, in order to show one of Liverpool's famous Green-Goddesses, as this route down Castle Street was soon to be re-placed by buses. Consequently a lot of the vehicles shown have a distinctive 1930s look. A Ford V8 Pilot and a Morris can be seen parked and a Scammell Mechanical Horse in L.M.S. livery heads towards Water Street. An E.R.F. truck travels in the opposite direction.

Train Spotters at Preston

This is definitely a scene close to my heart, as I spent many a happy hour on this platform on the south side of Preston Station. Train spotting was for some unknown reason banned from the station, so trying to avoid the Railway Police was all part of the game. This group of spotters is gathered round a Stanier Black 5, a mixed traffic locomotive built in the hundreds which could be seen working both goods and passenger trains from the London area right up to the north of Scotland. Let's hope the young spotters are left in peace!

Grosmont

Grosmont is the northern terminus on the North Yorkshire Moors Railway. The line was engineered by George Stephenson and opened in 1835. It closed in 1965. It re-opened in 1973 as a tourist line using preserved steam locomotives running between Pickering and Grosmont, and at certain times of the year trains run through to Whitby on the coast. Here we see one of the engine crew climbing aboard Standard Tank Engine No. 80135 prior to departing for Pickering.

Talbot Square – Yates Wine Lodge, Blackpool

A streamlined 'Vambac' tram stands beside the shelter on Talbot Square, Blackpool. Behind the tram is Yates Wine Lodge opened in 1868 as the Assembly Rooms also incorporating one of the first theatres in the resort. Sadly, it was burnt down in 2009. One of Blackpool's distinctive black and cream taxis is passing the tram and heading for the Promenade.

Maestro Moss at Le Mans

The Jaguar C-Type was one of the classic Le Mans sports cars. In 1953 form it was the first car to exceed 100 M.P.H. for 24 hours. Here the great Stirling Moss battles with a Cunningham during the classic race.

Morecambe 1950s

With its gently curving promenade and superb views across the bay to the Lake District, Morecambe has always been popular with day-trippers and holidaymakers. In the distance can be seen the Winter Gardens and the art deco style Midland Hotel, which has recently been refurbished and is back in business. As a child I remember visiting the resort in the 1950s and the novelty of riding on an electric train from Lancaster Castle Station. Here we see a Ribble Coach probably on a day trip from east Lancashire. The usual Fords and a Vauxhall can be seen as well as a motorcycle and sidecar.

Appleby 1950s – The Boroughgate

Like Stow-on-the-Wold, Appleby is famous for its annual Horse Fair, when the whole town is taken over and parking becomes impossible. A gypsy caravan can be seen, heading down the street and the driver of an early-style Landrover has stopped to have a chat with a local. Perhaps he's the owner of yet another Armstrong Siddeley, one of the earlier models finished in cream and burgundy. I visited Appleby recently and this scene has hardly changed.

On the Promenade Circa 1952

A summer's day in Blackpool during the 1950s. People are on the Promenade taking the air. A streamlined 'Vambac' tram introduced in 1939 and known as a Rail-Coach is heading down to the Pleasure Beach. Traffic heading north towards the Tower includes a horse-drawn landau, a Ribble Coach and a Rover. An Alvis followed by a Corporation bus head in the opposite direction. This is Blackpool as I remember it as a youngster.

Railway Montage

Several railway subjects are shown in this painting. The fireman and driver are seen on the footplate of a Standard Tank loco on the North Yorkshire Moors Railway. A fireman cleans out the smoke box of a Royal Scot loco, a dirty but necessary job to be done at the end of the day. Notice the coaling tower behind. The ash would be shovelled into a pit between the rails. The close-up view is of a coupling which belonged to an L.N.E.R. 0-8-0 locomotive at Grosmont Engine Shed on the North Yorkshire Moors Railway.

Skipton 1950s – The High Street and Market Place

From across the border a Guy Arab coach belonging to Lancashire United Transport conveys its passengers on a tour of the Dales. Also seen getting an admiring glance from a cyclist is an MG TD Midget, and alongside is a Sunbeam Talbot, and the usual Fords and Austins of the period. Fortunately, this view of the High Street with the parish church dominating the background has changed little in the intervening years.

Flying Scotsman and the Haymakers

Probably the most famous locomotive in the world, the *Flying Scotsman* achieved the first authenticated 100 M.P.H. in 1934. Designed by Nigel Gresley for the London & North Eastern Railway, here it heads its namesake train on its journey from London to Edinburgh in the 1930s. The horses and men haymaking take it all in their stride. The young boy with the dog is more enthusiastic. A Country Connections plate.

Trafalgar Square South Side

A showery day in the late 1950s. On the left is the National Gallery; to the right of the tree is the spire of St Martin's-in-the-Fields church completed in 1726. Dominating the background is South Africa House which was opened by King George V in 1933.

The traffic gets the green light to proceed into the top of Whitehall from West Strand. On the left is a silver Bentley with special coach work by Park Ward. A famous Routemaster is destined for Tooting. Next is an Austin FX3 London taxi. A blue Trojan van and a green Standard lead a RT-Type London bus which is followed by an Austin K8 van.

St Anne's Pier in the 1950s

St Anne's Pier was opened in 1885 and cost in the region of £30,000 to build. It was widened and extended in length to accommodate a Concert Pavilion a few years later. Parked outside the mock Gothic entrance are a fine selection of early 1950s cars including a green Riley Drophead, a Wolseley, a Standard Convertible, a Vauxhall taxi and a brown Vauxhall Velox. A Ford V8 Pilot stops at the Zebra Crossing.

W.H. Bowker Truck

This is a Leyland Beaver truck belonging to the Blackburn hauliers W. H. Bowker. This together with earlier and later models has been preserved and regularly attends transport rallies. I have depicted the vehicle as it would have looked in the centre of Blackburn just prior to the Second World War.

Darwen, Lancashire

The Lancashire town of Darwen lies a few miles south of Blackburn on the road to Bolton and Manchester. This view towards Bridge Street and Bolton Road is known as The Circus. The mock Tudor buildings on the right, known as The Criterion Buildings, housed the Midland Bank. The chimney dominating the town belongs to India Mill and was 255ft high. As well as the distinctive red livery Darwen Corporation bus, a two-tone Vauxhall Cresta complete with Whitewall tyres, a Bedford truck and van, as well as a Hillman Minx can be seen.

Le Mans – 24 Hour Race – Start 1954

I have had to use existing material, black and white photographs and some film footage on D.V.D. to create this painting but I felt this scene just had to be painted. At least I have seen cars such as the D Type Jaguar which Stirling Moss in the white helmet is about to leap into. Unfortunately, Jaguar didn't win: it was Ferrari's first Le Mans win.

Le Mans – 24 Hour Race – 1970

Times had changed for this classic motor race by 1970. The drivers no longer sprinted across the track to their cars; they were already strapped in when the flag fell at 4.00 p.m. It was a battle between the mighty Ferrari 512s and Porsche 917s and it was a Porsche win, their first of many.

Le Mans – 24 Hour Race – 1936

Nightime scene at Le Mans as an Aston Martin is refuelled in the pits.

Lytham 1950

Often referred to as Lytham St Anne's, they are in fact two separate towns which are divided by Ansdell and Fairhaven – all a bit confusing to the visitor, nevertheless, both lie to the south of Blackpool on the Fylde Coast of Lancashire. This is Clifton Street, a very attractive tree-lined shopping street, which still looks the same today, apart from the large white building in the distance, which was a cinema built in the art deco style. Unfortunately, this was demolished some time ago. The vehicles are very much pre-war style, a Wolseley heading towards us.

Donnington Park

During the late 1930s Germany dominated motor racing with the immensely powerful and seldom challenged Mercedes W125 and Auto Unions. The British E.R.A. was not really a contender for the German marque but here we see an E.R.A. and Mercedes doing battle at Donnington Park during what could be described as the golden age of the sport!

Chester – Bridge St 1950s

Most of Chester's main streets are now pedestrianised but not so in the 1950s. This view of Bridge Street is from the junction of Grosvenor Street. A two-tone Daimler makes stately progress. Behind is a Bradford van and across the street heading towards St Peter's church is a Jowett Javelin. Both the vans were built at Bradford by the Jowett Company.

Eastgate Street, Chester

The north side of Eastgate Street is featured here around 1950. The once familiar name of F.W. Woolworth has now gone as well as Kardoma. The clock was part of the celebrations marking the Jubilee of Queen Victoria. The actual archway dates from 1769 and replaced a medieval structure. This area is now pedestrianised so the traffic no longer has to squeeze through. The rear view is of an Armstrong Siddeley as it is passed by a black Jaguar Mark V. Buses, delivery vans and cyclists make up the scene.

Glasgow – Trongate

An ex-Liverpool tram, now in Glasgow livery, trundles down a snowy Trongate. This area known as Glasgow Cross used to be a very busy tram way junction. One of these ex-Liverpool trams now resides at the National Tramway Museum at Crich.

Glasgow 1950s – The Heilandman's Umbrella

This was the name given to the part of Argyle Street which ran under the tracks at Glasgow Central Station and contained shops which were permanently lit. The Glasgow tram system was extensive and was very well liked by the populace. It lasted till 1962. Fortunately, you can still ride on a Glasgow tram at the Crich Tramway Museum in Derbyshire. Also seen in this view are an Austin A35 van and a Wolseley.

Glasgow – Buchanan Street 1930s – 'Doon Buckie'

This is one of Glasgow's finest streets with a wealth of Victorian buildings many of them banks. It never saw trams so a double-decker bus can be seen together with an Austin and a Rolls Royce.

Classic Car Show – Near Garstang

A very pleasant way of spending a sunny Sunday afternoon is to attend a classic car show. These cars look well from any angle, not least rear views as seen here. From the left an American Hudson from about 1950, a two tone Austin and an Austin A40 from the early 1960s and a Bull Nose Morris complete the line up. Notice the different styles of head gear. Well it was a warm day!

Edinburgh – George Street 1950s

In many ways George Street seems secondary to its more famous neighbour Princes Street, but as can be seen from this view there are some very distinctive buildings together with statues and columns, which probably caused problems with traffic flow – and there is plenty of traffic to be seen here. Parked from the left are a Standard Vanguard, a Triumph Roadster, a Ford V8 Pilot and an Austin. In the foreground coming down the street is a Riley and further on the right in front of the Corporation bus is a Ford and an Austin, all highly collectable classics today.

Routemaster on Victoria Street, London

This 1950s' view shows a Morris Oxford and the rear of a Routemaster as they head along Victoria Street into Broad Sanctuary. The other Routemaster is passing Westminster Abbey with the tower of Big Ben rising up in the distance. A Leyland Hippo truck, a London taxi and an Armstrong Siddeley complete the scene.

Blandford Forum, Dorset 1950

Blandford Forum developed as a major market town in the eastern part of Dorset and it is now one of the best preserved Georgian towns in England. The majority of the buildings date from the early eighteenth century. Most earlier buildings were destroyed in two devastating fires. It's a summer's day in the mid 1950s and several interesting cars of the period are parked. From the left we spot an Austin A40 Somerset, a Singer Sports, a black Vauxhall and a Sunbeam Talbot. A smart yellow and black Rolls Royce dates from the 1930s, and a Fordson van is by the kerb making deliveries.

Blackpool Central Station 1950s

It's holiday time at Blackpool, an excursion train has arrived and its passengers are leaving the station, no doubt heading for a boarding house, hotel or café before venturing on to the Promenade, which can be seen in the distance. The tide seems to be out, exposing acres of golden sands. Various vehicles are included in this animated scene. Under the canopy are some taxis, one an elderly Rolls Royce. Following the Blackpool Corporation bus is a two-tone Ford Zephyr and a Morris. A white Jowett Jupiter, its top down, threads its way through the throng.

Belfast 1950s

A view of College Square East, as two trams pass. Tram No. 407 is a 'McCreary': they were delivered to Belfast in 1935 and they were a very comfortable tram. The other tram, a 'Moffett', dates from 1920. Both are painted in a distinctive blue and cream livery. Belfast lost its trams in 1954. A horse and cart, not uncommon in 1950s Belfast, passes a line of what would now be classics, including a Morris Oxford, Daimler, Wolseley and Morris 1000. The large tower belongs to the Assembly Buildings and cinemas were clearly very popular – there are three in this view.

Bradshawgate, Bolton 1956

This is probably Bolton's best known street which still carries traffic. The other main street, Deansgate, is now traffic free. The buildings here are rather a mixed bag of architectural styles. Pseudo black and white rubbing shoulders with tile and stone. Fortunately, the buildings still stand though some details have been removed on health and safety grounds. In the foreground heading towards us is a Scammell Scarab Mechanical Horse followed by a Morris van and a Bolton Corporation bus. A Morris 1000 Traveller is heading in the opposite direction. Cars on the right include an Austin A35, Hillman Minx and Bentley, and a two-tone Ford Zodiac complete with white-wall tyres and a blue Vauxhall Velox.

Fleet Street

Fleet Street is derived from the Fleet River which used to run close by. The street runs from the end of The Strand to Ludgate Circus, with St Paul's rising up in the background. Known for its newspaper offices, the clock belongs to the *Daily Telegraph*. Fleet Street lost much of its character when the newspaper publishers moved to Docklands. Once again pre-war RT's are evident as well as taxi cabs and a sleek Alvis.

Victoria Square, Bolton 1950s

Inspired by Leeds Town Hall and in the classical style, Bolton's was opened in 1873. At the time there was much debate about whether to have a clock tower as the cost would be around £7000. Today Victoria Square is a traffic free zone. Some attractive fountains are now to be seen and trees have been planted. These have rather taken over and a view of the Town Hall from this angle is almost impossible in the summer. A couple of buses head in opposite directions and the cars include a MK1 Ford Consul and an Armstrong Siddeley Sapphire.

Haymaking

Another very nostalgic scene from the turn of the century shows a local passenger train hauled by a London and North Western Webb 1P 2-4-2 Tank Engine passing a picturesque haymaking scene in the heat of summer. Such work would be very hard yet probably most satisfying, if the weather was fine. In later years many townspeople would combine their holidays with harvest work.

Blackburn Station – Looking West

An Austerity 2-8-0 locomotive brings a long rake of empty coal wagons into Blackburn Station. A lot of this coal traffic came west from Yorkshire and was destined for the mills and power stations of Lancashire. When I worked at the *Evening Telegraph* newspaper offices in Blackburn I would usually spend my lunch breaks on the platform watching these coal trains clanking eastwards. Usually in the company of my brother Michael who was a parcels clerk at the station.

Delivering the Milk

This was painted for a series of plate designs called 'Country Connections' and shows milk churns being delivered by horse and cart to the local railway station. As a perishable item milk was given priority treatment and was transported by express trains. It was first carried on the Liverpool and Manchester Railway in 1832 and milk traffic started on a large scale in 1865. Here churns are off-loaded from a horse-drawn cart onto a platform, as an ex. London & North Western 2-4-2 Tank Engine in L.M.S. livery gets up steam.

Cleopatra's Needle

This famous red granite obelisk situated on the Thames Embankment is over three thousand years old. First set up at Heliopolis in Roman times it was brought to Alexandria, presented to the British Government and was put on a vessel in 1877. Abandoned during a storm in the Bay of Biscay it was later recovered and landed in England in 1878. A bomb fell close by in 1917 and pitted the plinth with small holes. Similar Needles can be seen in New York and Paris. River-cruising paddle steamers pass by.

Longridge, Lancashire 1950s

This view of the level crossing in Berry Lane, Longridge is no longer to be seen, as the branch line closed in 1967. It was opened in the 1840s to serve a local quarry. Competition by bus caused the passenger service to be withdrawn in the 1930s. It is now the site of a mini roundabout but you can still see the station building. Here we see an Austin from the 1930s waiting for a goods train to pass hauled by a Class 7F 0-8-0 locomotive.

Crossing the Canal

A scene on the canal towpath where a horse drawn barge takes a well earned rest whilst a Midland Railway Express hauled by a Midland Compound locomotive crosses over the canal. Again this scene was part of the plate series 'Country Connections'.

Liverpool

A 'Sentinel' Steam Wagon towing a trailer at work in the Docklands of Liverpool soon after the Second World War. The Liver Building can be glimpsed between the dock crane and the warehouse.

Isle of Man Locomotive

This is Engine No. 11 Maitland. It is a Beyer Peacock 2-4-0 Tank Engine and runs on the 3 foot gauge Isle of Man Railway. It is seen here at Port Erin which is at the western end of the 15 ½ mile line from the capital Douglas. One of my memories of this delightful railway is of standing on the tiny platform at Ballabeg and actually being able to stop the train by raising an arm.

Bowness 1930

To give it its full name, it should be called Bowness on Windermere. The town of Windermere was a tiny farming hamlet until the railway arrived in 1847. Bowness just down the road and next to the lake was called by ancient settlers Bulness because the land that jutted out into the bay looked like a bull's head. This view of the pier with its pleasure steamer yachts and distant Langdale Pikes is taken from what is now the 'Belsfield Hotel' built for the Baroness of Sternberg in 1845. In 1869 it was bought by industrialist H. W. Schneider who used to commute to his factory at Barrow-in-Furness via his own steam launch to Lakeside and then by private railway carriage to Barrow. This 1930 view harks back to a time when parking was a lot easier and free. The cars are a mixture of Austins, Fords and a Bull Nose Morris.

Downham, Lancashire

Downham is a very attractive village near Clitheroe in Lancashire. It owes its unspoilt beauty to the Assheton family who have been in the village since 1558. To preserve its unspoilt character Lord Clitheroe installed an underground cable system so there are no T V aerial. This makes it an ideal location for period T V dramas and it has been used several times, one of the most recent being *Born and Bred*. The small car parked by the stream is a 'Bond' Three-wheeler. They were made locally at Preston. It was powered by a chain-driven two stroke motor which was mounted on the single front wheel which also steered the vehicle. Because of its low weight and lack of reverse gear the holder of a motor-cycle licence could drive it without taking a driving test.

Lower Briggate, Leeds 1950s

A 'Horsfield' car No. 158 is about to turn into Duncan Street on its way to Meanwood. The Horsfields were widely known as 'Showboats' after a popular musical entertainment. The first of the class No. 151 was built at the Kirkstall Road Works in 1930. It had seating for 23 inside and 37 upstairs. Car No. 160 acted as the official last car when the system closed on 7 November 1959. Car No. 180 survives at the National Tramway Museum. A Standard Vanguard is on the left and a green Morris 1000 is on the right, both examples of early post-war car design.

New Market Street, Leeds – Circa 1950

A Horsfield car in the early blue livery is en route No. 8 to Elland Road. The route which originally went beyond Elland Road to Moreley was converted to bus operation in June 1955 but received a temporary reprieve in 1956 as a result of the Suez crisis. The blue livery was replaced by the red colour scheme later in 1950.

Westminster Bridge, May 1952

London lost its trams in July 1952. This scene shows an E/3 tram built in 1930; it had upholstered seating and could seat 74 passengers, 28 in the lower saloon and 46 in the upper. Its destination is Woolwich via Kennington. Heading north across the bridge and at the foot of Big Ben is a new RT bus followed by a Scammell Scarab Mechanical Horse in British Railways livery, and behind that a luxurious Daimler 2½ litre sports convertible with bodywork by Barkers of Coventry. Coming in the opposite direction and about to overtake the tram is a Jowett Javelin.

The Square, Stow-on-the-Wold 1955

This is the west end of the Square complete with Market Cross and the fifteenth century tower of St Edward's church. This was once a bustling wool centre but because of its position set high on a hill the railway never got there so it never achieved the size of other similar towns such as Cirencester. Nevertheless many roads met there and as can be seen a fine collection of classic cars are parked in the Square. Among them a Triumph Roadster, Austin Somerset, Vauxhall, Triumph Renown and an Armstrong Siddeley Sapphire in two-tone blue. To the right of the two horses is a Morris 1000 Traveller and a pre-war Rover is leaving the Square.

Market Place, Garstang

Situated on the River Wyre, Garstang's reputation for its fine market goes back to the fourteenth century. The stone pillar topped with an orb marks the site of the original cross and stands on a medieval base: erected in 1754 it was renovated in 1897 to mark Queen Victoria's Diamond Jubilee. Beyond the cross stands the Town Hall, its clock tower topped by an intricate weather vane. Both the Lancaster Canal and the main West Coast Railway are close by as are the A6 and M6 roads. Unfortunately, Garstang Station has now gone. Two vehicles to note in the scene are an early Landrover which is parked up and on the right is a Sunbeam Rapier Series 3, a car produced by Rootes Motors in 1960.

Fleetwood

The Pharos Lighthouse was built to guide shipping down the channel of the River Wyre to be aligned with the lower Lighthouse and as can be seen was situated in the street. The trams passed the Lighthouse for the first time in 1925 when the new terminal loop line was built. A 'Balloon' double decker tram built by English Electric in 1934 will soon be heading back down the coast to Blackpool. The advertising boards on the right conceal the bowling green which could be seen from the top deck of the tram. In front of the garage is a Morris 1000 and following the Ford Anglia is a Bedford C A van built by Smiths Delivery Vehicles of Gateshead. The Cornette range was specially made for the ice cream trade.

Market Street, Manchester circa 1930

This view looking down Market Street towards The Royal Exchange building captures the variety of traffic that could be seen during this period. In the foreground a Standard tram heads towards Piccadilly. The old trams finished in 1949, but a new system called The Metrolink was opened in 1992.

Tower Bridge and the Pool of London [Aerial View]

This view looking east gives one a good idea how the river winds its path eastwards towards the sea. In the lower left we can see part of the Tower of London and beyond that is St Katherine's Dock and the Tower Hotel. A lot of the original warehouses were destroyed in an air raid and were pulled down to make way for re-development. Only one original warehouse together with its bell tower and Dock Master's House remain standing today. Beyond is Wapping with the London Docks. These docks became a vast storehouse for a multitude of different cargoes including wool, rubber, spices, ivory and coffee. In the early '60s the Wapping Entrance Lock was filled in and by 1969 London Dock had closed. On the opposite bank we get a glimpse of Surrey Commercial Docks and part of Southwark. To the right of Tower Bridge is Butler's Wharf and Courage's Anchor Brewhouse built in 1895. It closed in 1981 and the buildings were converted into luxury apartments.

Lambeth Bridge

The present bridge seen here was erected in 1929. It replaced an earlier suspension bridge of 1861 which was found to be unable to take the increasing weight of motor traffic. That first bridge had replaced a ferry which was known to have sunk whilst carrying Oliver Cromwell's coach in 1656.

County Hall at Westminster, late 1970s

In contrast to the Gothic majesty of Westminster Abbey and the Houses of Parliament, the London County Hall on the opposite bank of the river is in the Renaissance style and was opened in 1922. Here a Routemaster double-decker passes over Westminster Bridge heading south.

Pall Mall

Pall Mall in the heart of the West End is home to clubs such as the Athenaeum and The Royal Automobile Club. On the right is Waterloo Place, then the 'Guards Memorial' the pedestal of which was placed there in 1859, the figures being cast in bronze from a captured Russian cannon. The left hand statue seen here is of Florence Nightingale erected in 1913. Traffic sweeps past on the one-way system. Of note are a Jaguar and two Rolls-Royces – well it is 'clubland'.

Piccadilly Circus, London Circa 1950

Six of London's streets meet at Piccadilly Circus. This viewpoint is from Regent Street looking across to Coventry Street, which leads into Leicester Square. The turning on the right is Haymarket, and the beginning of Shaftesbury Avenue can be seen on the left. Alfred Gilbert's memorial to the Earl of Shaftesbury shows Eros firing an arrow.